2x(12/09)7/11

2x 12/09 √12/12

BW

SEP 2 3 2008

Forensic Ballistics: Styles Of Projectiles

by Sue Hamilton

VISIT US AT
WWW.ABDOPUBLISHING.COM

Published by ABDO Publishing Company, 8000 West 78th Street, Suite 310, Edina, Minnesota 55439.
Copyright ©2008 by Abdo Consulting Group, Inc. International copyrights reserved in all countries.
No part of this book may be reproduced in any form without written permission from the publisher.
ABDO & Daughters™ is a trademark and logo of ABDO Publishing Company.

Printed in the United States.

Editor: John Hamilton
Series Consultant: Scott Harr, J.D. Criminal Justice Dept. Chair, Concordia University St. Paul
Graphic Design: Sue Hamilton
Cover Design: Neil Klinepier
Cover Illustration: iStockphoto
Interior Photos and Illustrations: p 1 Laser trajectory, AP; p 3 Simulated gunshot wound to the arm, Corbis; p 4 Rocket launch, iStockphoto; p 5 Bullet fired from gun, Corbis; p 6 Flintlock, iStockphoto; p 7 Dunhuang silk banner, Wikipedia; p 8 Bow Street Runner, Mary Evans; p 9 Flintlock firing and musket ball, John Hamilton; Bullet Mold, iStockphoto; p 10 Hollow point bullet, Photo Researchers, Inc.; p 11 Rifling inside cannon barrel, AP; p 12 Revolver and bullets, iStockphoto; p 13 Firearms examiner, AP; p 14 .22-caliber handgun, iStockphoto; Rifling patterns, courtesy FirearmsID.com; p 15 Firearms examiner, Getty Images; p 17 Forensic scientist uses Bulletproof computer program, Photo Researchers, Inc.; p 18 Thompson submachine gun, iStockphoto; Frank Gusenberg, Corbis; p 19 Crowds form after the St. Valentine's Day massacre, Corbis; pp 20-21 St. Valentine's Day massacre reenactment, Corbis; p 22 Calvin Goddard, courtesy Forensic Technology; p 23 (top) Police with Thompson submachine guns, Corbis; (bottom) Gangster with Thompson submachine gun, Corbis; p 24 (left) J. Edgar Hoover, Library of Congress; (right) 1930s FBI Lab, FBI; p 25 FBI agent, Corbis; p 26 Gunshot residue, courtesy Georgia Bureau of Investigation; p 27 Testing for gunshot residue, Photo Researchers, Inc.; p 28 Bullet holes in steel, iStockphoto; p 29 Bullet trajectories, Getty Images; p 31 Bullets, iStockphoto.

Library of Congress Cataloging-in-Publication Data

Hamilton, Sue L., 1959-
  Forensic ballistics : styles of projectiles / Sue Hamilton.
     p. cm. -- (Crime scene investigation)
  Includes index.
  ISBN 978-1-59928-990-8
  1. Forensic ballistics--Juvenile literature. 2. Firearms--Identification--Juvenile literature. 3. Bullets--Identification--Juvenile literature. 4. Criminal investigation--Juvenile literature. I. Title.
  HV8077.H27 2008
  363.25'62--dc22
                        2007035160

CONTENTS

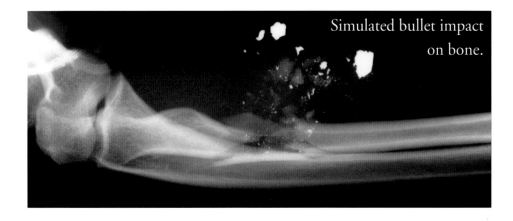

Simulated bullet impact on bone.

Ballistics and Firearms Identification

Below: Ballistics is the science that studies the motion of projectiles, such as the path of a rocket or missile.

In the United States, 60 million people own 200 million firearms. Most of these weapons are used legally, but many become part of crime scene investigations. Scientists skilled in forensic ballistics analyze evidence from the use of firearms and bullets in crimes.

Ballistics is the science that studies the motion of projectiles. While a projectile may refer to anything that is forcefully moved through the air, such as a rock or ball, usually this science follows the effects of a bullet or rocket. The word "forensic" is defined as using science and technology to investigate a crime and provide facts in a court of law.

There is a gun for every 10 people on Earth. Each year, 10 to 14 billion rounds of ammunition are produced— enough to shoot every person in the world twice. In 2004, according to the Federal Bureau of Investigation (FBI), 11,344 murders and 164,998 aggravated assaults involved the use of a firearm. It's easy to see why law enforcement agents need the science of forensic ballistics.

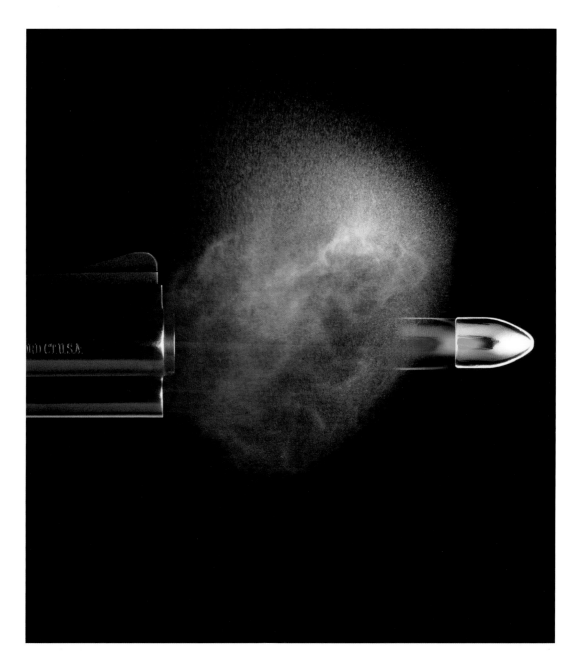

Crime analysts may also refer to this science as firearms identification, examination, or comparison. These specialists help figure out if a bullet or bullet casing came from a specific gun, and where the shooter was located when the weapon was fired. Science, math, and firearm knowledge are combined to determine who did what at a crime scene.

Above: A bullet is fired. Ballistics specialists can often tell if a certain bullet came from a certain gun.

The History Of Ballistics

The first explosive powder was invented in China around the ninth century. The Chinese may have used it for launching fireworks. However, explosive powder was soon used against invading armies by launching rockets from bamboo tubes. Development continued, and metal gun barrels were created. By the 1300s, the Chinese had created the first handheld, long-barreled firearms known as muskets.

Not long afterward, the weapons were carried to the Middle East, and then to Europe. By the 1600s, Europeans had created lighter muskets with improved firing mechanisms. Firearms became tools of law enforcement, but also weapons of murder. Police needed to be able to match a victim's gunshot wound to the gun that fired the bullet, but forensic ballistics was in its infancy.

In 1794, a man was shot and killed in Lancashire, England. During the autopsy, the doctor pulled a bullet, as well as paper wadding, from the victim's body. At the time, the process to load a rifle was to put gunpowder in the barrel, drop in the round lead bullet, then top it off with a small wad of paper. Everything was tapped down. When the gun was fired, both the bullet and the paper shot out of the gun. In this case, both the bullet and paper ended up in the victim's body. A suspect named John Toms was arrested, but what proved his guilt was a sheet of paper found in his pocket. The wad of paper taken from the victim's body was an exact match to a spot ripped out of the paper in the suspect's pocket. Officers knew they had their man.

Below: A flintlock pistol.

Above: An early gun, known as a fire lance, and a grenade are shown in the upper right corner of this ancient Chinese silk banner. Created in the 10th century, the banner was discovered in Dunhuang, a city in north central China. The banner is believed to be the earliest surviving illustration of firearms. By the 1300s, the Chinese had created the first handheld, long-barreled firearms known as muskets.

Above: A member of the Bow Street Runners, London's first professional police force.

In 1835, Englishman Henry Goddard was a member of the Bow Street Runners, London's first professional police force. The Bow Street Runners were founded in 1745. They traveled throughout the nation to arrest criminals. Goddard's job as a detective brought him to the scene of a burglary in Southampton, on the south coast of England. Thieves had reportedly broken into a home and shot at the household's butler as he lay in bed. Goddard carefully dug out the bullet from the bed's headboard. The detective examined it and noticed a small flaw marking the outside of the bullet. Since people molded their own bullets at the time, the detective also checked out the butler's pistol and bullet mold. The mark on the bullet matched a flaw in the butler's mold.

No one had broken in. The butler had tried to rob his employer, shooting his headboard as a way to draw attention away from himself. Faced with the evidence, the man confessed—the butler did it.

Detective Goddard earned the distinction of being the first person to trace a bullet to a specific gun. Firearms identification had begun.

Above: A flintlock rifle is fired.
Below: In the 1800s, people molded their own bullets. The mold often had small scratches or marks. These flaws appeared on the bullets, making it possible to tell what mold was used to make a bullet.

Rifling Patterns

Muskets are smoothbore weapons, which means the inside of the barrel—the part that the bullet travels down—is smooth. The round musket ball fits loosely inside. When the gun is fired, the ammunition bounces from side to side until it emerges from the barrel. The bullet's bouncing motion greatly decreases the weapon's accuracy.

By the 1800s, manufacturers started using rifling to replace smoothbore barrels. Rifled barrels have spiral grooves cut on the inside. Bullets also changed shape. Longer extruded bullets, which cut through the air more effectively, replaced the old, round projectiles.

Below: A hollow-point bullet after being fired from a rifle. The rifling pattern from the weapon's barrel appears as stripes on the outside of the bullet.

These new firearms and bullets were not only more accurate, they were more identifiable. When a bullet travels down a weapon's rifled barrel, the ammunition's soft metal picks up the design of the rifling, which differs from weapon to weapon. For crime investigators, these rifling patterns are like having the gun owner's signature right on the bullet.

In 1889, Professor Alexandre Lacassagne of the University of Lyon, in France, sought to identify a murderer from a bullet pulled from a victim. The police had detained several suspects and seized their weapons. Lacassagne, an expert in forensic investigations and studies, noted that the bullet used in the murder had seven grooves. The scientist found a perfect match among the confiscated weapons. Its owner was arrested, tried, and convicted of murder. For the forensic scientist who knew what to look for, the weapon and the bullet pointed directly to the murderer.

Above: A rifling pattern is clearly displayed on the inside barrel of this 105mm cannon. Large or small, most firearms since the 1800s have had these kind of spiral grooves cut inside the barrel. The grooves greatly increase a weapon's accuracy. Ballistics specialists are often able to tell if a bullet was fired from a certain weapon based on the rifling pattern that has been transferred to the soft metal of the bullet or the bullet casing.

What Type Of Firearm Was It?

Back in the 1800s, firearms manufacturers cut rifling patterns into the barrels of their weapons using their own custom tools. The barrels were handmade, which means each one was slightly different and identifiable.

Below: A snub-nose .38 Special revolver with bullets. Measuring a weapon or bullet's caliber (size) is one of the first steps in identifying it.

Modern manufacturers use precision machines to build firearms. How do today's firearms examiners identify a bullet fired from a specific weapon? The fact is, fired bullets and cartridge cases are still like fingerprints—no two have exactly the same markings. Some experts call this a "mechanical fingerprint."

To determine if a bullet or cartridge casing came from a specific gun, forensic scientists begin by figuring out the general class of the firearm. Then they try to match individual characteristics of the weapon.

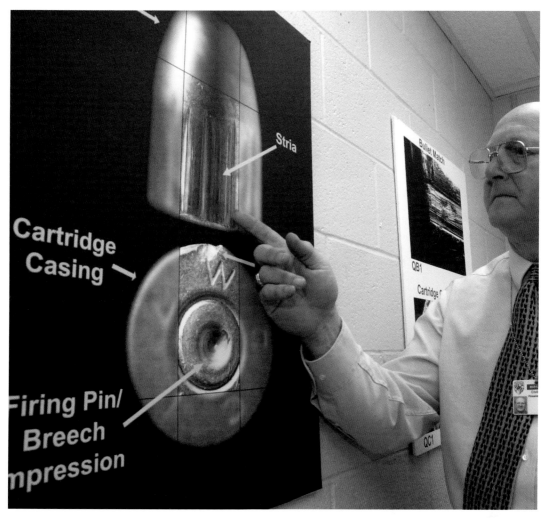

Above: Firearms expert Joseph Kopera points to the area on a bullet that will be used by the Integrated Ballistics Identification System (IBIS), a computer database that helps identify guns by examining bullets fired from them.

Class Characteristics

Class characteristics are features that are common to all firearms within a certain class, or group. The first steps in identifying a firearm, bullet, or cartridge casing is to identify the weapon's caliber, then the rifling pattern, and then the general marks placed by manufacturers on cartridges.

Caliber

A simple measurement provides an investigator with a weapon's caliber. Caliber is the internal diameter (the distance from one side to the other) of a firearm's barrel. Caliber also indicates the corresponding diameter of the bullets and casings used in the weapon. For example, in the United States, a bullet that is 22 hundredths of an inch (.56 cm) in diameter is called a .22-caliber bullet. Firearms and bullets that are manufactured in countries using the metric system are usually measured in millimeters.

Above: A .22-caliber handgun.

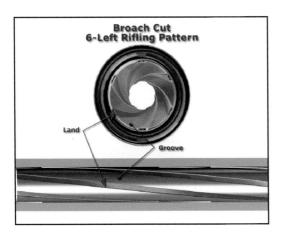

Broach Cut
6-Left Rifling Pattern

Land

Groove

Button Rifled 16-Right
"Micro-groove"
Rifling Pattern

Land

Groove

Rifling

Gun manufacturers create their own standard rifling patterns. A gun barrel begins as a solid rod of steel. A hole is drilled down the center of the rod, then the rifling is formed in the barrel. Once finished, the barrel is patterned with grooves and lands—the areas that are raised up between the grooves. Firearms examiners check the lands and grooves to see how many grooves there are and whether they spiral to the left or right. Some common rifling patterns are 4/right, 5/right, 6/right, 6/left, 8/right, and 16/right.

Left: Two common rifling patterns used by manufacturers in gun barrels.

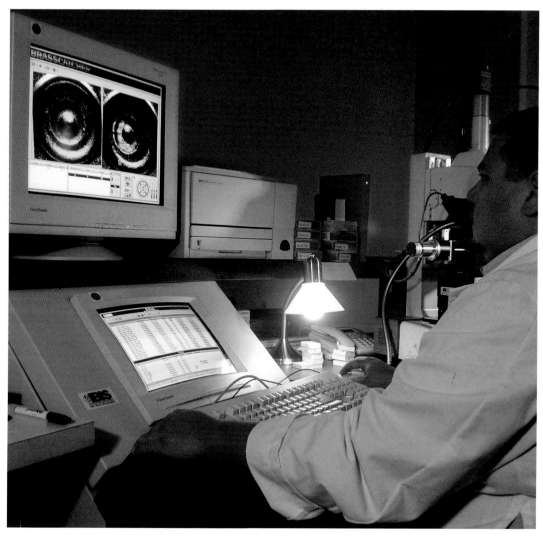

Above: A forensic scientist in a crime lab examines a shell casing with the aid of a computer. A computer database links police department crime labs around the country and greatly speeds up the matching of ballistic evidence.

Cartridge Cases

Firearms leave microscopic marks on the metal shell casing, the part of the cartridge that contains the propellant (such as gunpowder or cordite). For example, any individual firearm leaves breech face marks, firing pin impressions, extractor marks, and ejector marks on the casing. Some of these marks are unique to the weapon's manufacturer, and allow for general firearms identification.

Finding the Exact Weapon

While size, rifling, and general casing marks may identify a type of weapon, the next step in a crime scene investigation is to determine if a fired bullet or casing came from one specific weapon. Firearms technicians look at the marks that come from a specific weapon, bullet, or cartridge casing. These individual characteristics may be caused by the manufacturing process, use, or damage.

Individual Characteristics
Striations

Striations are microscopic scratches that are imprinted on bullets or cartridge casings. Since the inside of every gun barrel has its own mechanical fingerprint, all bullets shot from a particular weapon have the same unique striations imprinted on them. This assumes that the gun is not damaged or altered in some way.

Comparison Microscope

If a weapon has been retrieved by investigators, a test bullet is fired into a water-filled tank or boxes of cotton waste. This test bullet is then compared to a bullet retrieved from a victim or a crime scene. Examiners use a comparison microscope to look at both the test bullet and the crime scene bullet side-by-side.

The bullets are mounted on a rotating microscope stage that lets firearms experts look at the entire surface. First they search for the most obvious markings, called striations, on the evidence bullet. When that is found, the bullet is locked into place. Next, they search for the same marks on the test bullet. If similar markings are located, technicians magnify the markings to an even greater size.

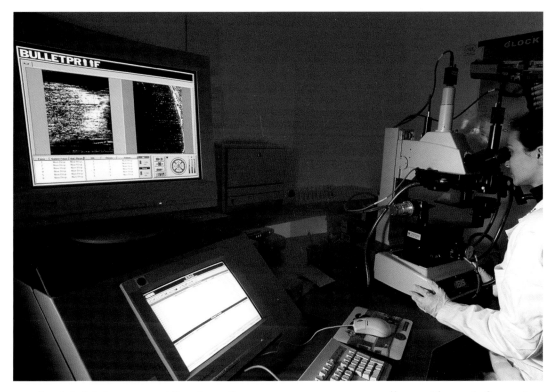

At this higher magnification, firearms experts can usually tell whether or not both bullets were shot from the same gun. If so, a photomicrograph is taken by the comparison microscope. However, even bullets that are shot one right after another may have slight differences in their striations. Sand, dirt, gunpowder residue, and many other outside factors could alter the look of two bullets. Finding a match is a painstaking process.

Above: A forensic scientist compares markings on bullets using a microscope and a computer program called Bulletproof.

Computers Assisting Firearms Experts

Today, computer programs such as IBIS (Integrated Ballistics Identification System), Bulletproof, and Drugfire assist firearms experts. Close-up videos are shot of bullets and/or cartridge casings. The videos are digitized and loaded into a computer database. The computer program checks for similarities between evidence and test firings. Experienced technicians then review the noted markings and determine whether or not there is a match.

"Nobody Shot Me"

Above: A Thompson submachine gun. *Below:* Gangster Frank Gusenberg lived for 3 hours after being shot 22 times, but refused to say who shot him.

In 1929, on a bone-chilling St. Valentine's Day morning in Chicago, Illinois, gangster Frank Gusenberg lay bleeding on the floor of a garage surrounded by six other dead or dying companions. When a police sergeant asked Gusenberg who shot him, he whispered, "No one… Nobody shot me." Police had to find the answer that the dying gangster refused to tell.

The St. Valentine's Day massacre was a gruesome challenge even for experienced Chicago police officers. Witnesses reported seeing a police car arrive at the SMC Cartage Company at 10:30 A.M. on February 14, 1929. Two or three men in police uniforms and two men in plainclothes entered the red brick warehouse. Not long after, gunfire erupted inside the building. Minutes later, two men marched out of the warehouse with their hands in the air, followed closely by uniformed men with machine guns. The group drove off in the squad car. It seemed that an arrest had taken place. But a terrified dog howling inside the building led a neighbor to investigate further.

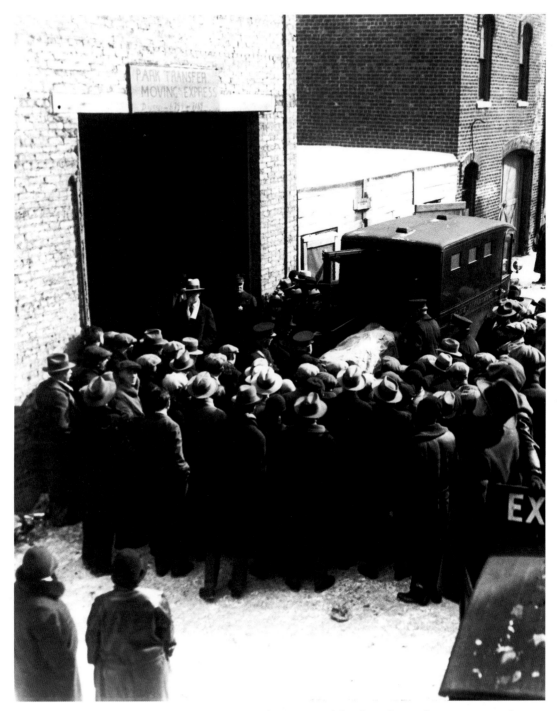

Above: Crowds form as police remove the victims' bodies from the garage at the SMC Cartage Company in Chicago, Illinois. Seven people were murdered by a rival gang on February 14, 1929. It became known as the St. Valentine's Day massacre.

Inside, six members of the George "Bugs" Moran gang and one unlucky mechanic lay side by side, red rivers of blood running from their bodies. Each man had been shot several times in the back. The neighbor's frantic call brought prompt response by the Chicago police.

By studying the crime scene and interviewing witnesses, police quickly pieced together what had happened. Gangsters dressed as police officers had entered the warehouse and ordered the seven men to turn around and line up against a wall. The men did as they were ordered because they thought they were being arrested for selling illegal liquor. The disguised hit men then opened fire.

Moran gang member Frank Gusenberg, despite receiving 22 bullet wounds, lived for three hours. In a misplaced sense of honor, the dying victim refused to identify the killers, reportedly saying, "I ain't no copper." Most people believed that the massacre was a "hit" by famous mobster Al Capone's rival gang. Other people wondered if members of the Chicago police force had actually killed the gangsters in cold blood. Law enforcement turned to science and technology to help find the murderers. Dozens of bullets and bullet casings were collected from the crime scene. Forensic ballistics and firearms comparison would become a vital part of the investigation.

Above: A reenactment of the St. Valentine's Day massacre. Six gangsters of the George "Bugs" Moran gang and one unlucky mechanic were lined up, expecting to be arrested by police officers. However, the police officers were actually disguised hit men, who murdered the rival gang members by shooting them in the back.

Identifying the Murder Weapon

Above: A firing pin imprint on a shell from a tommy gun.

In 1929, seven bullet-ridden bodies and 70 gun casings were collected from the St. Valentine's Day massacre crime scene in Chicago, Illinois. The bullets and casings came from .45-caliber Thompson submachine guns. Also known as tommy guns, the weapons were favored by both law enforcement and criminals for their compactness, large bullets, and automatic firing ability. Calvin Goddard, a ballistics pioneer and investigator who helped establish America's first independent crime lab in New York City, was brought in to identify the murder weapons.

Below: Ballistics pioneer Calvin Goddard.

Goddard began by test firing all eight of the Chicago police department's Thompson submachine guns. Using the newly invented comparison microscope, Goddard compared the evidence bullets and casings with the department samples. None of the striations matched. This proved that no police weapons were involved in the killings. The Chicago police were cleared of wrongdoing. Now the real police work began—searching for the murderers and their weapons.

Above and Below: In the early 1900s, both police and gangsters used tommy guns.

Months later, police raided the home of Fred "Killer" Burke, a known hit man for gangster Al Capone. Among Burke's arsenal of weapons were two Thompson submachine guns. Police turned the evidence over to Goddard, who test fired the weapons and compared the bullets and casings to those found at the crime scene. They matched. Goddard's firearms identification confirmed that these submachine guns were the same ones used in the gruesome February 14 slayings.

Burke, along with two other Capone gunmen, Jack "Machine Gun" McGurn and John Scalise, were charged with the massacre murders. Burke was convicted and served time in prison. Scalise was murdered before his case went to trial. McGurn beat the charges, but was himself murdered February 15, 1936.

As a twist of fate, the St. Valentine's Day massacre resulted in the opening of an independent Chicago crime lab. Forensics scientist Calvin Goddard, with the help of several businessmen, established the Scientific Crime Detection Laboratory, which was originally associated with Chicago's Northwestern University. The lab conducted ballistics and firearms identification, as well as fingerprinting, blood analysis, and trace evidence tests all in one place. J. Edgar Hoover, head of the FBI, was so impressed with Goddard and his lab that he asked for the scientist's help in establishing the FBI's own crime lab in 1932.

Below: J. Edgar Hoover, director of the FBI from 1924 to 1972, was so impressed with the forensic work of Calvin Goddard that he asked for the scientist's help in setting up the FBI's own crime lab in 1932.

Today, the Firearms-Toolmarks Unit of the FBI examines hundreds of cases involving firearms, ammunition, and cartridge cases, and trains law enforcement personnel in firearms identification, gunshot residue analysis, and trajectory analysis.

Left: An FBI agent examines a block of ballistic jelly. The substance reacts like human flesh, helping ballistics specialists determine how far bullets can travel into a body.

Gunshot Residue

The microscopic particles that escape when a weapon is fired are called gunshot residue (GSR). GSR analysis uses a scanning electron microscope to identify the unique metals found in a fired weapon's residue. The goal is to identify a shooter based on the residue found on the person's hands or body. However, it's extremely easy for a person who has nothing to do with a firearm to be contaminated by a recently shot weapon's GSR.

Simply being in an area where a firearm is discharged, shaking hands with someone who fired a weapon, or even sitting in a police car, can cause particles to land on an innocent person. *Forensic Science International* stated that tests conducted at the Institute of Criminalists in Prague, Czech Republic, show that particles remain in a closed room up to eight minutes after a shot is fired. The study determined that "…someone entering the scene after a shooting could have more particles on them than a shooter who runs away immediately."

Although GSR tests are still conducted on suspects, positive tests are usually used as only one part of a criminal case. A positive test is frequently questioned in court. Many lawyers and defendants convince judges and juries that the findings are the result of accidental exposure.

Below: When a weapon is fired, smoke from the gunpowder surrounds the hand of the shooter, leaving gunshot residue.

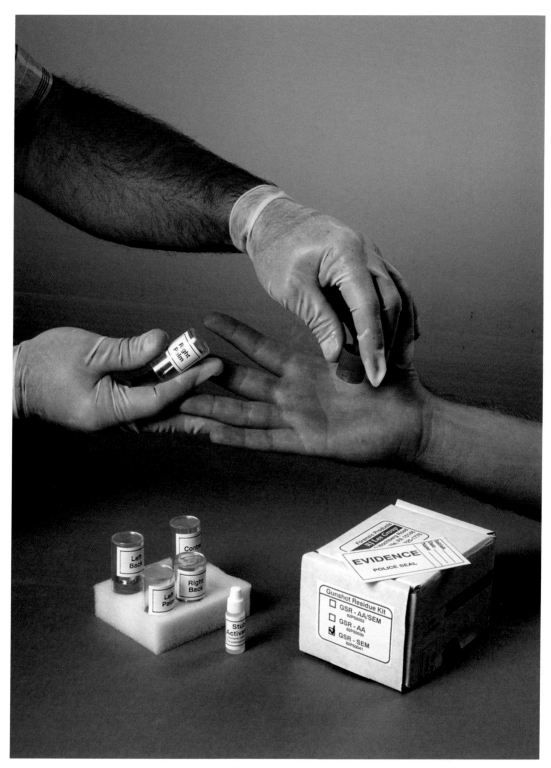

Above: A suspect is tested for gunshot residue.

Trajectory Analysis

Trajectory is the path that a projectile or object follows when moving under a certain amount of force in certain conditions. Forensic scientists analyze bullets and bullet impacts to determine where a weapon was fired, and sometimes by whom. This can become quite complicated, especially when several people with similar weapons are involved in a crime scene.

Below: Bullet holes in steel. Ballistics specialists study how fast, far, and deep bullets travel through the air, and through different materials.

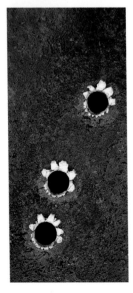

Many factors are involved in how a projectile is analyzed. *Internal ballistics* looks at the type of gunpowder that sets the bullet in motion, as well as how the bullet travels through the barrel of a firearm. *Exterior ballistics* takes into account how fast a bullet travels through the air, as well as its trajectory or path. *Terminal ballistics* looks at how hard a bullet hits, as well as how deep a bullet travels into its target. A ricochet—when a bullet hits and rebounds off one or more surfaces—is also an important ballistics factor.

For example, a recent British case involved the firing of a gun in a roomful of people. The shooter claimed that he'd fired the gun at the floor. If so, the man would be guilty of an illegal discharge of a firearm. However, if he had purposely fired into the crowd, he'd be charged with a much more serious crime, one that might result in a long jail term. Lucky for the shooter, the investigator searched and found the complex trajectory the bullet traveled.

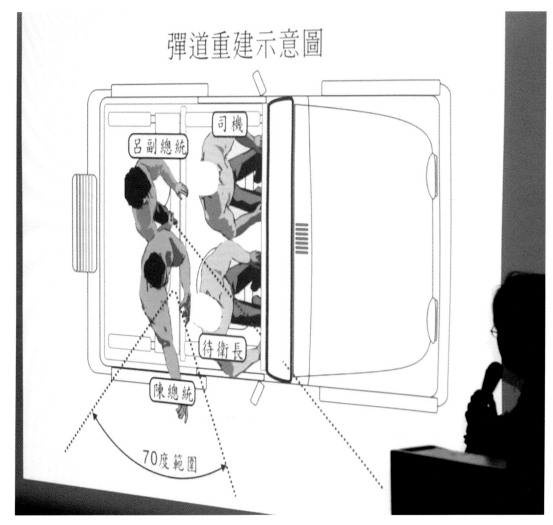

彈道重建示意圖

司機

呂副總統

待衛長

陳總統

70度範圍

After being shot, the bullet ricocheted off a metal piece on the floor, traveled up a side wall, ricocheted off the ceiling, struck a table leg, then ricocheted once more, finally finishing its trajectory into an unlucky person in the crowd. The man received the lesser charge.

Forensic ballistics is a complicated and technical science, but one that is frequently used to provide proof of a suspect's guilt or innocence. From identifying a murder weapon with a bullet or bullet casing to finding a shooter in a crowd of people, forensic ballistics is one of the most important tools used by crime scene investigators.

Above: A forensic scientist discusses a shooting in Taipei, Taiwan. Investigators wondered if the attempted killing was staged, but the bullet paths show that the shooting was real.

GLOSSARY

ARSENAL — A collection of guns owned by a single person, military group, or country.

AUTOPSY — An exam performed on a dead body to find out the cause of death.

BREECH FACE MARKS — When the explosive powder inside a cartridge begins to burn, the cartridge case is sent backwards against the breech face of the gun. The microscopic marks on the breech face are then transferred to the cartridge case. These marks are known as breech face marks.

CARTRIDGE — The ammunition for a firearm that contains a bullet, plus a casing that holds a propellant such as gunpowder or cordite.

CARTRIDGE CASE — The outside cylindrical container that holds together a bullet, powder charge, and primer. Commonly made of brass, it may be made of other metals as well.

CORDITE — A smokeless powder used to propel bullets.

DEFENDANT — A person, business, or government entity (such as a corporation or town) accused of doing something wrong. In a court trial, defendants try to defend themselves against the charge or charges placed against them.

EJECTOR AND EXTRACTOR MARKS — When a cartridge case is automatically removed from a firearm's chamber, fine marks from the weapon are produced on the cartridge case.

EVIDENCE — Objects, and sometimes information, that helps prove the details and facts in a legal investigation.

FIRING PIN IMPRESSIONS — When a weapon is fired, the firing pin strikes the primer of the cartridge, creating microscopic impressions that are unique to that weapon.

FLAW — A mark that mars the surface of an object.

HIT MAN — A person paid to kill another person.

PROJECTILE — An object that is moved through the air using force. This usually refers to objects fired from a weapon, such as bullets or arrows, but it can also mean such things as balls or rocks.

TRACE EVIDENCE — A small but measurable amount of evidence, such as gunshot residue.

Above: The effects of bullets of all calibers are studied by ballistics specialists.

INDEX